SIMPLE CHIC

PARIS

SIMPLE CHIC

HERRON

EFFORTLESS

ORGANISED

SLEEK

INVITING

FRESH

INTIMATE

Discover your simple chic style. With five exciting substyles to explore in this book, you'll never be short of ideas and inspo.

THE SIMPLE CHIC VIBE

A simple, peaceful outdoor area in which minimal styling meets maximum nature.

In today's busy world, with most of us juggling multiple balls and then some, home is a sanctuary – or it should be. A welcome refuge, where the stresses of the day can be set aside.

The simple chic home sets you up perfectly. It provides a clean, minimalist, beautiful aesthetic in which functionality and comfort are given equal but high priority. In this ordered environment, where everything has a place, we can establish peace and harmony.

In this book, you'll learn about five different expressions of the simple chic home – each one has a slightly different skew to suit varied tastes. There's Scandi chic, an extension of the ever-popular Nordic style; farmhouse chic, where yesteryear meets tomorrow; mid-century chic, a stylish reinvention of the iconic look; boho chic, the globally inspired, luxurious style; and the hot-button Japandi style, where East meets West in a display of earthy minimalism.

MINIMALIST FURNITURE

Select a few quality pieces to showcase your minimalist approach. Where form meets function is the sweet spot. Emphasise clean lines and free yourself from unnecessary clutter.

NEUTRAL COLOUR PALETTE

White (and shades of white), beige, grey and soft pastels make the perfect backdrop to the simple chic home.

SIMPLE CHIC ESSENTIALS

POPS OF COLOUR

Think colours inspired by nature for accent wall finishes (paint, wallpaper, wall textures), statement furniture, upholstery, soft furnishings and decor.

NATURAL TEXTURES

Use natural textures for hard and soft furnishings. Think jute for rugs, wicker for furniture and decorative items, and linen and cotton for throws, curtains and cushions.

NATURAL MATERIALS

Use natural materials in the home, including stone and wood.

STATEMENT ART PIECES

Large canvases fill blank walls with high impact, while smaller collections on shelves and surfaces create a curated gallery feel.

CONTRAST

Pair natural woods with black metals, matte with glossy and patinated finishes, curved with straight shapes, and heavy with light materials to strike the balance between cosiness and functionality.

LAYERED LIGHTING

Boost natural light where possible and complement this with task lighting and accent/mood lighting, including wall sconces, picture lights, floor lamps and table lamps.

STYLES WITHIN A STYLE

Discover your perfect expression of simple chic home style by exploring the five substyles outlined in detail in this book.

SCANDI CHIC

The ever-popular Nordic style gets a fresh look with the layering of simple chic elements.

Page 27

FARMHOUSE CHIC

The traditional country or farmhouse look eschews its frilly edges, opting for a fresh reinvention in this bang-on-trend home style.

Page 65

MID-CENTURY CHIC

This iconic style gets the dial turned down a little in its simple chic form – but it's still a great choice for those who love colour and personality.

Page 99

BOHO CHIC

Coastal home owners will gravitate to the boho chic style, where low-slung couches make a comfy spot from which to view the global treasures on display.

Page 141

JAPANDI

A perfectly balanced East-meets-West style, where minimalist and earthy cohabit with functional and cosy to create a calm, easeful home.

Page 175

Can Scandi get any better? It's already a beloved approach to home styling, but as you'll discover, with the additional focus on chic elements, yes, it can get even better.

SCANDI CHIC

◂ Blond woodwork combined with a neutral colour palette is iconic of Scandi chic design.

It's cold and dark in Nordic countries and that fact alone has determined much about how the Scandinavian design style came into being, notably its emphasis on light-filled but cosy living.

Scandi chic is all about amping up that sense of airiness, so let in the light and open up spaces where possible. Declutter the home to create order and, by extension, calm.

A neutral colour palette of cool whites and greys makes for the perfect backdrop, while materials used in the home should have a natural vibe – think blond timber and earthy fibres such as rattan, cane and jute.

Celebrated for its simple, clean lines, uncluttered spaces and reliable-at-heart functionality, Scandi design also embodies the essential notion of *hygge*, or comfort. Functionality, simplicity and beauty are cornerstones of Scandi chic style.

STYLE HIGHLIGHTS

LIGHT, OPEN SPACES

Perhaps due to the darkness of the northern latitudes, Scandi design has evolved to let in the light. Think clear, open spaces, large windows lightly covered, if possible, and living spaces oriented towards the light.

LIGHT, NATURAL TIMBERS

The use of blond timbers and timber finishes is classic in Scandi design, and it can feature in furniture as well as flooring and shelving and kitchen or bathroom cabinetry.

BLACK AND WHITE ELEMENTS

Black and white is commonly incorporated in Scandi design with dramatic effect. Consider using it as a design feature in artworks or furnishings such as pendant lighting.

UNCLUTTERED SPACES

A place for everything and everything in its place is central to Scandi interior design. Consider how to use storage effectively to keep surfaces clear, and stay on top of unnecessary clutter.

CONTRAST

A key principle in Scandi design, contrast can be introduced in multiple ways. Think old and new elements, light and dark, functional and cosy items, straight and curved lines, hard and soft furnishings.

LOVE OF NATURE

Welcoming natural elements into the home is a beautiful way to create warmth, character and life. It's a case of plants and more plants, but also consider natural textiles and textures in furnishing and furniture.

Keeping it light, white, bright and natural are guiding principles for the backdrop to your Scandi chic home. From there, just add personality.

THE CANVAS

▸ White walls, grey concrete flooring and timber ceiling boards combine to create the perfect Scandi chic canvas.

To successfully achieve the Scandi chic look in your home getting the blank canvas right is key and, fortunately, it's pretty easy to make it happen.

Focus your energies on creating a bright, light and neutral backdrop as this will be the starting point from which you introduce your personal style. Use paint in white and shades of white, or neutrals (beige, tan or greige). A fresh coat of paint on walls and ceilings does a lot to set the right tone.

Also bear in mind floors and wall coverings – keep these light in order to let in the light. If plans and budget allow, consider introducing elements of timber and concrete to help create the sense of clarity, light and connection to the natural world that is characteristic of the style.

Neutral backdrops, black and white elements and pops of colour that are inspired by nature just about nails the Scandi chic colour palette.

COLOUR PALETTE

The Scandi chic colour palette boasts a wonderful combination of simplicity (a muted backdrop) and personality (you can add your personal touches).

The neutral backdrop can be white (or shades of white), but tones of grey, beige or tan will work too. For simplicity's sake select one tone for the paint colour and then layer natural tones in your choice of furniture and furnishings.

The iconic Scandi black and white can be introduced in artwork, furniture, furnishings or kitchenware. Use it sparingly for a subtle look, or for extra drama consider black (or black-and-white) furniture or features such as kitchen bench or splashback tiles.

Pops of colour add personality and warmth in the Scandi home – think colours inspired by nature, such as moss or sage green, blush pink, pebble grey.

▲ This Scandi chic bedroom scene artfully combines a neutral backdrop with crisp whites and pops of colour.

With calm at its core, the mood of the Scandi chic home is established by the principle of hygge – a cosy atmosphere among friends, let's say.

MOOD

▸ Order, neatness, a lack of clutter and an abundance of light is where it all starts, creating calm in the home.

It's all encapsulated in the one word: hygge, a Scandinavian term that is hard to pin down precisely in English, but suggests a cosy, happy mood created through a combination of a comfortable environment and the convivial company of friends and family.

Hygge is a blend of these elements, and its intimate vibe can be found in, for example, the glow of candlelight, a reading nook, dimmer lights, cosy cushions and throws, or books that invite you to pick them up and stay a while.

A soft colour scheme, natural light and natural elements are important in hygge too, as they help to create a mood of effortless calm that's conducive to the type of intimacy and connection that hygge invites.

The Scandi chic focus on functionality as well as comfort creates an environment that's perfect for living together harmoniously.

SHARED SPACES

Scandi chic spaces are ideal for sharing, as they boast harmonious and organised rooms with minimalist furniture, soft textiles and a calming colour palette. These features help to create an organised home, which feels stress-free, easy and cosy.

Kitchens are functional, clean and free of clutter, providing the perfect environment for share households or families to conduct their culinary tasks with minimal disruption and maximum enjoyment. Likewise, bathrooms in this style are clutter free and well organised, with a premium placed on effective storage and creating a space that's functional as well as aesthetically pleasing. In both spaces, artwork and plants are definitely not out of place. These elements add the hug in the hygge of these shared spaces.

▸ A clutter-free dining area makes for a harmonious home.

Less is more in Scandi chic decor. A few carefully chosen, well-crafted items will hit the right note in your home.

DECOR

▾ Bunny tail grass in an earthenware vase makes for a beautifully simple decorative piece.

Decorative elements are often used sparingly and chosen with intention, even precision, in the Scandi chic home. Every item should be functional or beautiful, if not both at the same time.

Scandi chic decor reinforces a sense of calm in the home, often drawing on the naturally calming effects of nature to achieve that. Selecting decorative objects, artwork or furnishings that make use of colours and textures from the natural environment will help you to achieve this look and feel in the home. Curved shapes exude forms of nature too, and are commonly found in this home style.

Don't be scared to introduce the occasionally quirky item – personality is allowed and will help soften the look.

So far as budget allows, selecting a few items that are well chosen is better than having 'more stuff'.

The trick to nailing the Scandi chic look in your home is to effortlessly combine simplicity with a sumptuous, cosy feel.

FURNISHINGS

While the Scandi chic interior might appear a little stark on the surface of it, don't be fooled. Comfort is king and ought to be a key consideration in your choice of furnishings.

As with decor, a few quality items is a great way to go. In making your choice, consider quality, design and comfort, and how the piece fits into your broader design scheme. Aim to connect colours, textures and pattens across different spaces of the home.

Natural textiles, such as wool, cotton, silk, cashmere and bamboo, are perfect choices for different types of furnishings in the home. Add these in layers to create warmth and cosiness.

A thick woollen rug feels wonderful underfoot; complement with a smaller sheepskin for that Nordic look – use on the floor or as a throw over a chair.

▲ The boucle fabric on this armchair is a popular choice in the Scandi chic home.

A sense of pared-back sophistication is the mood that will be created by your careful curation of Scandi chic style elements.

MOOD BOARD

Set the tone for your mood board by deciding first on your background colour palette – will it be crisp white, a shade of white or warmer neutrals? Also consider how much of the classic Scandi black and white you'd like to introduce and whether that will be in hardware, furniture, decor or soft furnishings. Will you include brighter pops of colour, and how these will be introduced?

Build up your mood board by incorporating your preferred decorative objects in the Scandi style. Remember the 'less is more' and 'quality over quantity' mantras when it comes to decorative objects, and place comfort and function centre-stage when making your choices. Sense-check the items on your mood board against your chosen colour scheme.

◂ A neutral palette, plenty of white and blond timbers set the scene in Scandi chic.

▸ Consider curves – they add a lovely softness and natural organic vibe to the home.

▾ Plants are always in place in the Scandi chic home, especially large leafy ones like monstera.

◂ Scandi chic functionality is on display with this beaded curtain tie-back.

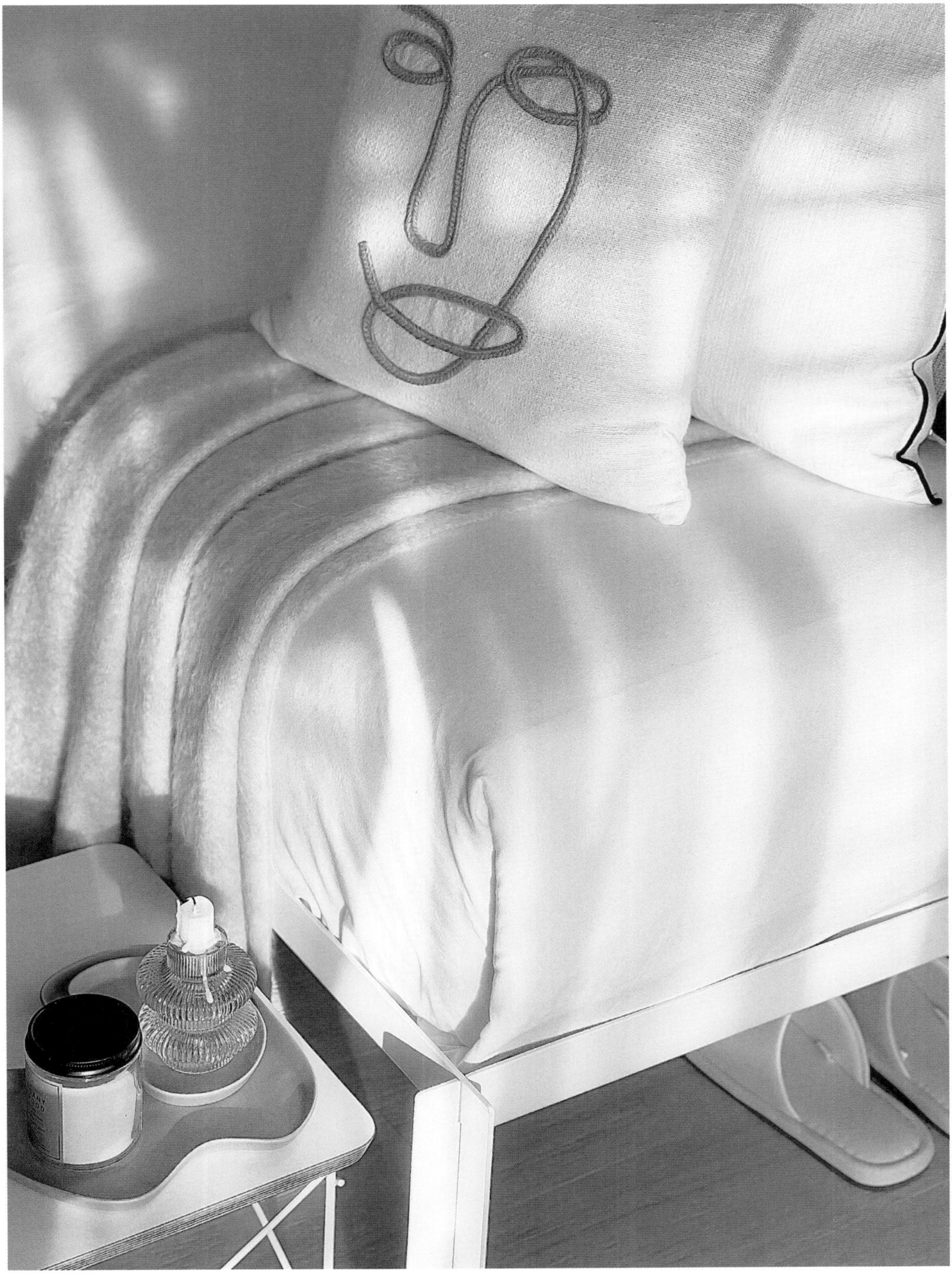

Handmade vases in organic shapes, featuring greenery or dried grasses, are the perfect decorative addition to the Scandi chic home.

Simple but comfortable and inviting sets the tone for this Scandi chic outdoor room.

Presenting small displays of items connected by colour is a great way to achieve a clean, consistent look.

A super-chic Scandi-style kitchen is bright, white, light and clutter free.

Small details, such as organic bed linen and earthy vases of flowers, add the hygge in this bedroom.

When the classic rural homestead gets a modern makeover, you have one of interior design's hottest trends: farmhouse chic (but no farmhouse required!)

FARMHOUSE CHIC

▸ Sleek lines and glossy finishes mark out the chic in this country-styled dining room.

Forget fusty floral tablecloths and great-grandma's quilts, the modern version of farmhouse is oh-so-chic and oh-so-stylish. It's a homage to the past – with honest materials and good craftsmanship at its heart – and to the present, with a minimalist approach to furnishings and decor, and a Scandi-inspired approach to functionality and organisation in the home.

At the heart of the home, there is likely to be a table – an island bench in the kitchen for informal cuppas and a large dining table for communing with family and friends. The dining table is a centrepiece – it's a place for joy and connection with others. Be expansive (as big a table as the space reasonably allows) and choose chairs for comfort as well as style – hopefully you'll linger there a while.

STYLE HIGHLIGHTS

HONEST MATERIALS

Incorporate plenty of timber, stone and metal. Wooden elements can take the form of distressed timbers, shiplap or VJ panelling, barn doors, reclaimed wood and exposed wood beams.

RUSTIC REBRANDED

Cool, clean and refined — rustic elements are balanced with crisp, contemporary styling.

COSY AND STYLISH

Large, comfortable pieces of furniture, such as couches and armchairs and, of course, a central dining table, are an invitation to kick back and watch the sunset, with a good book or the company of family and friends.

VINTAGE OR ANTIQUE ELEMENTS

A sizeable portion of the 'chic' in this style is introduced with the inclusion of these elements – think pitchers, milking stools, farmhouse utilities, prints, photos or local maps, mason jars and hats.

NEUTRAL COLOURS WITH DEEPER ACCENTS

Farmhouse chic depends on a base of whites and neutrals, layered with deeper colours such as chocolate, greens and blues. Plants and greenery are used as accents.

SHELVING AND CABINETRY

Open shelving bursting with kitchenware, plants and flowers is iconic of trad farmhouse style. In the chic variation, items on display may be fewer and simpler, and shelving is supplemented by bespoke cabinetry, where budget allows.

Natural materials and earthy tones combine to create a soulful backdrop in the farmhouse chic home.

THE CANVAS

▾ A fireplace is both a luxury and a surefire way to deliver the farmhouse chic look.

This chic, contemporary take on the traditional farmhouse style seeks to emphasise natural light, where possible creating bright spaces that seamlessly connect the indoors and outdoors. Carefully chosen lighting, including overhead lights, wall lights and feature lighting, plays an important role too in creating a fresh, modern-looking home.

This style of home pays homage to the old-fashioned values of good bones in a home, fine craftsmanship, and the use of honest materials (wood, stone, concrete, glass and metal). Combining these materials in a confident but unassuming way is key to creating the right backdrop on which to style up your farmhouse chic home.

Let nature be your guide in selecting the base palette for your farmhouse chic home. Add your favourite colours in small doses for the finishing touches.

COLOUR PALETTE

Colour is key. Starting with a neutral base is ideal – whites and greys create a calm backdrop and allow for the introduction of pops of colour. When choosing these accent colours, look to nature for clues. Think the green shades of eucalyptus trees; oranges and yellows that evoke rusty farmyard metal, the red dirt of the outback or natural pigments like ochre; and muddy blues that bring to mind a creek at sunset, or a slate tile.

Colour can be introduced in a variety of ways. For higher impact, walls, carpets or rugs and window coverings are important to consider. But colour can also be introduced in more subtle ways, such as through choice of soft furnishings, artwork or even coffee-table books on display. For best results, pay attention to these details.

▲The warm chocolate tones of this sheepskin rug are an invitation to relaxation.

There's a respect for nature, home and family that's integral to this home style – and the mood is love.

MOOD

▸ This lounge scene is simple but comfortable and inviting.

The mood is soft and welcoming. The vibe is unpretentious comfort. The values are honesty and integrity. The energy is soulful, and the promise is timeless. Farmhouse chic style embodies all of this, seemingly without effort. These core values are blended with a simple, minimalist aesthetic to create a version of farmhouse style that feels fresh and contemporary at the same time as it is warm, homely and nostalgic.

Farmhouse chic represents a subtle shift from the traditional. Floral, fussy and over-cluttered makes way for clean lines and contemporary styling, with items on display chosen with precision. The consistent use of materials and colour tones delivers a warm and inviting spirit – even though you may be nowhere near a farm.

Utilitarian but comfortable and homely is the hallmark of the farmhouse chic home.

SHARED SPACES

Shared living spaces in the farmhouse chic style are an interplay of practicality, comfort and detail.

The practical is rarely the glamorous side of styling, but paying attention to it will pay dividends, ensuring the home is functional, streamlined and organised.

Farmhouse chic homes, especially those actually in the country, tend to see a bit of wear and tear (and they usually have a dog or two on the loose), so considering furniture and upholstery that will stand up in the face of that is important. Think blankets, throws, slips and cushion covers that are easy to replace and clean. Mudrooms, boot rooms and drying rooms are all a necessary part of managing the elements in outback country life, and these practical elements have made their way into the broader look and feel of the style. Even in smaller spaces, a mudroom can make for a practical and stylish inclusion.

▲ The farmhouse-style dining table is just as appropriate in farmhouse chic as in the traditional version of the style.

Whether vintage or contemporary, carefully chosen decorative pieces tell a story and set the mood.

DECOR

▸ The classic farmhouse sink looks up-to-date thanks to the stylish cabinetry surrounding it.

It is important to get the right balance between clutter and character. It's tempting to display all of your good-looking utensils, crockery, vases and books. Keeping daily items to hand does make sense, but be sure to limit yourself to items that you genuinely use on a regular basis. The farmhouse chic look is 'on display' but not cluttered – it's a delicate balance so take care with it.

Display chosen items that articulate your style and fit in the theme of farmhouse chic – natural fibres, earthy tones, wood, tarnished metals and, of course, flowers, fruit and greenery. Think baskets and hats, greenery and bunches of flowers, stacks of carefully chosen books on the coffee table and handmade ceramics or knitted throws on display. Don't forget to include vintage pieces, family or local memorabilia which will add warmth and personality to the home.

It's all about comfort. Easy furnishings in natural fabrics and materials add a luxurious warmth to the farmhouse chic home.

FURNISHINGS

With the basics in place, and comfort embedded in your furniture choices, it comes down to deciding on the furnishing details that will help articulate your farmhouse chic home style.

Soft furnishings such as curtains, cushions, rugs, throws, bedding and table linen provide an opportunity to add warmth and personality to the home. Layer your soft furnishings for maximum comfort and visual appeal. Stick with simple and plain, in muted tones, or opt to add a splash of colour, such as a brightly coloured quilt.

Alongside the need for a robustness of furnishings, the importance of lighting in country style should not be overlooked. Mood lighting can create a cosy ambience on dark and cooler evenings.

▸ The vintage-style metal pendants make a style statement in this kitchen.

There's an expansiveness to the farmhouse chic home which, coupled with quirky vintage design pieces, can create a bold, individual look.

MOOD BOARD

The tone is set through the use of traditional materials at the heart of the home. Timber (reclaimed and new), stone and metal (such as brushed nickel, pewter and brass) feature prominently in the structure and finishings of the farmhouse chic home.

A next dimension is added through the use of natural textures and materials like leather, jute, hemp and linen in fabrics and furnishings. These provide a softer finish to complement the wood, metal or stone foundations and fittings.

A neutral colour palette with darker accent colours that are inspired by nature defines the spaces, while oversize rugs add style and resilience to tough timber floors that historically absorb heavy feet.

Decorative items are carefully chosen and limited in number compared to in the traditional farmhouse style. They can be vintage or new, according to your preference.

▲ The rustic rebrand is on song in this organic timber bedhead.

▶ Pewter cutlery adds a beautiful vintage touch.

▲ Thicker stripes adds a fresh, contemporary feel to the home.

▶ A cute and chunky farmhouse-style stool can double as a coffee table.

◀ A fluffy sheepskin adds warmth underfoot, while daisies add a burst of farmhouse sunshine.

A very traditional sink setting in honest materials is complemented by chic tiling and mirror.

Keeping displays simple and elegant, such as these stems in two identical vases, hits the mark in farmhouse chic.

WILD
FREE

Consider using mismatched chairs to add personality and enable you to blend old and new in your dining space.

The focus is on comfort and character in this farmhouse chic living space.

A 'volume-down' version of the original style is still sufficient to create a mid-century chic home that's full of warmth and bursting with colour and personality.

MID-CENTURY CHIC

▾ This classic mid-century chair makes a bold statement.

The pinnacle of cool and a favoured style choice for urban hipsters, mid-century style has been given a subtle tone down in this style to make it accessible for the rest of us.

Its hallmark features of bold colours, curved shapes and geometric lines, and the use of diverse materials that include wood, metal, glass and vinyl, have been retained but quietened, as the more minimalist chic aesthetic is overlaid.

Mid-century style is chic by nature, so it's a question of degrees. You might want to introduce just one key piece of furniture as a nod to the style, and complement this with more contemporary pieces. Or restrict bold colours and geometric patterns to accent pieces rather than on walls and flooring. As with the simple chic style in general: less is more.

STYLE HIGHLIGHTS

ICONIC FURNITURE

Low-slung couches and armchairs, crescent-shaped couches: the mid-century era produced iconic furniture pieces that remain popular today, such as the Eames chair and Saarinen tulip tables.

TACTILE FINISHES

It's all about the touchy-feely when it comes to mid-century finishes. Consider boucle, leather, velvet and suede as options for couches, chairs and soft furnishings.

CLEAN LINES AND STREAMLINED FORMS

Mid-century chic style emphasises 'clean lines', focussing on linear and geometric shapes and patterns in the architecture and interior design of the home.

ORGANIC AND GEOMETRIC SHAPES

The curved lines, bends and spirals inspired by nature are shapes and patterns commonly found in the mid-century home. They can feature in furniture, furnishings, decor and print.

MIXED MATERIALS

Traditional materials like wood (usually mid to darker tones such as walnut) are paired with 'newer' materials such as metal, glass, vinyl, plexiglass and plywood. Creating contrast is key to the look.

VIBRANT COLOURS

While neutral colours (like beige and white) are frequently used in this design style, it also embraces bold, contrasting colours. Think mustards, teals, oranges and olive greens.

Think clean, streamlined design with plenty of personality showing through in the use of colour, pattern and decor choices.

THE CANVAS

◂This bold exterior wall, fronted by juicy succulents, is iconic of mid-century chic.

Sleek lines, bold colours and geometric patterns are essential to creating the mid-century chic look at your place.

To achieve this look, avoid any unnecessary embellishments or detailing in furniture. Instead opt for streamlined finishes, tapered legs, cabinets and drawers with smooth, flush finishes. The choice of natural woods like teak, walnut and rosewood for hardware helps to emphasise this clean and elegant look.

Incorporate patterns, such as circles, triangles, diamonds, herringbone and other symmetrical shapes in your home's canvas – in wallpaper, tiling, splashbacks or flooring.

Colour is key in mid-century chic, and here's where you can really have some fun. Read on.

Mid-century chic home style affords a rare chance to celebrate bold colour. Pick what you love and go for it.

COLOUR PALETTE

One of the best things about mid-century chic is the freedom it allows to be bright and bold with colour. Most colours have a place in the style, but particularly popular are olive greens, mustard yellows, burnt orange and chocolate brown. And pops of cherry red and teal are not out of place either.

In the traditional form, these bold colours can be used any which way – on walls, ceilings or floors, on furniture or in decor and furnishings. Bold colours and patterns can confidently be paired together, too. In the chic variation of the style, you could consider offsetting one or two bold colours against plenty of white or neutral, which will ensure light and space are prioritised as well as pop and personality.

It's up to you how far to push colour in your home – it's personal – but one thing's for sure, in the mid-century chic style you have plenty of options.

▸ This kitchen bench goes boldly in it's colour choice, but is nicely offset by white cabinetry, benchtop and paintwork.

It's warm and welcoming, with high vibes that are conducive to conversation and connection. The mood is joy.

MOOD

Mid-century design emerged in a historic moment of post-war optimism. Austerity gave way to the exuberant use of colour and pattern, confident use of contrast, and the introduction of cheeky shapes and fun decorative elements. The net result? A dynamic, forward-thinking environment in which all of these elements were employed to stimulate, entertain and create a fun home environment, full of life and soul.

Depending on your specific choices, this mood can be toned down or turned up, from warm and nurturing to energetic and emotionally stimulating.

Taken as a whole, mid-century chic, with it's quirky, bold design approach, creates a rich, warm and welcoming mood in the home.

◂The bold, geometrically patterned wallpaper creates the mood in this mid-century-styled bedroom.

With its focus on purpose as well as presentation, the mid-century chic home creates eminently livable spaces.

SHARED SPACES

Living spaces in the mid-century style are commonly open plan, with living, dining and kitchen spaces tending to flow together as part of one continuous interior space. This reflected the emerging casual and relaxed lifestyle of the time, a trend which endures today.

While mid-century modern furniture is undeniably beautiful in its simplicity, it is also all about functionality. Furniture and hardware is selected for its purpose as well as for its aesthetic. The focus on clean lines, functionality and the absence of clutter (trinkets and ornamentation are normally kept out of sight) helps to create an environment that is harmonious for people to enjoy together.

▲The lounge setting in this living space is the perfect blend of contemporary comfort with mid-century style.

It's definitely the fun part – choosing decorative items for your mid-century chic home is where you get to serve it up and showcase your unique style.

DECOR

▸ The table and chairs in this dining space are iconic of the mid-century style.

Lighting is a good place to start when introducing decorative elements to your mid-century chic home, because functional is beautiful after all. Traditional starburst or rod and ball lighting has its place if you love it, but white paper lanterns or standing lamps are good chic substitutes. Wall lights are great for ambience, and well-chosen table lamps afford an opportunity to introduce the iconic curves and colours characteristic of this design.

Soft furnishings such as rugs and cushions with the bold geometric patterns and colours of the era are easy ways to introduce the look.

Artworks, whether large-scale bright paintings, framed prints or black and white photos, have a significant role to play in this design scheme. Mirrors, too, are the perfect functional-but-decorative item.

Elegant, sophisticated and stylish. That's the goal, and a well-chosen combination of furniture and furnishings will help you nail it.

FURNISHINGS

Keep it chic and elegant: think low-slung chairs with tapered legs and boucled sofas with rounded backs. There's something about that lower centre of gravity that exudes cool and sophistication.

Coffee tables and dining tables in geometric or organic shapes and crafted in mixed materials such as glass with wooden or metal frames serve up the retro feel, while in the bedroom simple, minimalist frames with jewel-coloured bedding drive home the look.

When selecting bedding or soft furnishings, choose textured fabrics like wool, tweed or corduroy, plain or patterned, which are emblematic of mid-century design. Velvet can add a luxurious touch, or to tone things down stick with natural fibres in more muted tones. Plants help to soften the look and breathe life into the home.

▲ This bedroom is virtually glowing, thanks to the colour and pattern, lush greenery and rich wooden tones.

Go bold or go gently, with a mood board that packs a colourful punch or makes a quiet nod in the direction of mid-century chic.

MOOD BOARD

To deliver your version of mid-century chic in the home, first decide on how hard you want to go on 'the look', and then tailor your mood board accordingly. If you are not totally committed, then consider introducing colour and pattern in soft furnishings and wall art, which are replaceable. But if you want a bold look then a feature wall or splashback is perfect to showcase some stylish geometric patterns. Consider investing in one statement piece of mid-century-styled furniture, perhaps a couch or table, which can really help set the tone for your chosen style.

Beyond that, have fun selecting decorative pieces and soft furnishings in the style to complement your home and create a look you love.

▸ Breeze blocks are iconic of mid-centrury design.

▾ This sweet collection is set off nicely against the deep rust colour scheme.

▴ Pops of bold colour add the joy to mid-century chic homes.

▾ Terrazzo marble floor or tiling (the real thing or vinyl) is having a moment.

◂ Mid-century chic does not have to be colourful. If that's not your vibe, let the materials, like the timber of this dresser, do the talking instead.

A feature fireplace is stylish and practical, providing warmth in wintertime and a focal point for the room all year-round.

The simple sphere wall light in this bathroom scene hits the perfect mid-century chic note.

Iconic mid-century furniture provides the centrepiece, but the overall style of this room is cool, uncluttered and elegant.

Curved shapes and natural materials make a subtle nod to mid-century in this chic kitchen.

Mid-century-style furniture establishes the look in this lounge room.

In boho chic, the global influences and personal expression of 'boho' meet the clean lines and slick finishes of contemporary home style.

BOHO CHIC

▼A globally influenced aesthetic combined with the clean lines of contemporary furniture is typical of boho chic.

Bohemian, or boho, interior design has its roots in the hippie culture of the '60s and '70s. We've come a long way since then and the current iteration of the style – boho chic – maintains many of its original and eclectic characteristics while bringing it up to date with the inclusion of fresh, contemporary elements.

Boho style traditionally draws inspiration from nature and from global cultures, making it a good match for free-spirited souls. Rattan, macrame and ethnic patterns would not have been out of place in the style then and they still aren't, but it's not uncommon nowadays to match this with plush rugs, sleek finishes and high-gloss surfaces such as countertops and polished floors. Boho chic is all about a masterful blend of modernity and classic elements in furniture, furnishings and decor.

One thing remains the same, and that is the highly individual nature of this style, where the only rule is there are no rules.

STYLE HIGHLIGHTS

RESORT FEEL

With a bright, white, airy, resort feel, the dream of a sunlounger and a margarita is never far away in this style.

NEUTRAL PALETTE

Boho chic is all about a light and white base, mixed in with grey, beige and bone hues. It's starkly elegant and beautiful, pared back and quiet in tone.

PLANTS ARE PRIMARY

Multiple plants in different sizes and positions, plus artwork inspired by plants and nature, are absolutely on point in this style.

LAYERED

Whether it's a marriage of muted patterns or a cosy combination of neutral textiles, boho loves layers. Think soft blankets thrown over a ladder, a beaded pendant hanging from a wooden beam, patterned rugs over reclaimed floors.

WOVEN TEXTURES

Bring warmth to the neutral colour scheme by adding plenty of textures: woven floor rugs (or woollen carpets), fluffy throws and textural pillows. Rattan, wicker and seagrass feature in decorative pieces such as baskets or mirrors.

INSPIRED

The boho chic home tells an inspirational story about its owner through the display of items relating to personal experiences, opinions and travels.

Bright, white, light and airy is the ideal backdrop on which to style your boho chic home.

THE CANVAS

▸This dining space is bright, light and uncluttered – but somehow full of stories.

The canvas is the easy part. You are aiming for a very bright, light and almost white backdrop against which to style your boho chic home.

High ceilings and large windows are a gift if you are lucky enough to have them. Regardless though, pay attention to lighting and window coverings. High ceilings can afford longer and larger pendant lighting, whereas lower ceilings may need spots to create the brightness associated with the style. Window coverings should be simple and elegant – sheers are a good option. Floorboards are a great fit with the boho look and if you are able to paint them white, all the better. Painted white concrete floors or tiles look wonderful, too.

In creating your boho canvas, it's important to pare back. Declutter where you can and specifically remove anything that's too colourful or clunky. You want a nice clean blank canvas on which to create your beautiful boho home style.

Take Mother Nature's lead with a colour palette that honours the resplendent variety and myriad hues of colour in the natural world.

COLOUR PALETTE

The boho chic colour palette is inspired by all that Mother Nature has to offer – the creamy whites, bright sea-spray whites, earthy neutrals (think clay, bone, tan, beige), dirt reds, river-pebble blues and moss greens. Bringing these colours centre stage into your home will help set the tone for the boho chic look.

Consider adding texture to colour too – raw-earth-style finishes to paintwork add an earthiness that hits the right note for this design style.

If you want to add in some bolder colour elements, that's fine too. Consider picking a bright colour that continues the connection with nature – bright sunshine yellow for example, or burnt orange. You can also experiment with introducing colours at opposite ends of the colour wheel as these shades should complement each other.

▸ If you're stuck for a splash of colour, plants will always answer the call.

COOKBOOK

To some extent the mood is what you make it, as this is a highly individual style in which your choices tell your story.

MOOD

◂ The mood in this kitchen is fun and joyful with a dose of Med vibes.

With a look and a vibe that's reminiscent of a tropical resort, the boho chic home is a place where relaxation is a priority. The mood is chill, with a side of 'salon', where it's the order of the day to sit back with friends sharing stories of travel adventures.

There's a free-spirited aesthetic that dominates in this home style, expressed through natural textiles and fibres, plants, macrame wall hangings, comfortable seating, soft-under-foot luxurious woollen rugs and a celebration of the natural world that exists within the home and just outside of it.

An absence of clear structure to this style gives it a certain charming warmth and anything-goes feeling. The inclusion of personal mementoes and storytelling items in the decor helps to entrench this sense of individuality in the style.

Boho chic homes are designed to share; with a resort vibe that invites relaxation and connection, delivered by furniture and furnishings that demand to be enjoyed.

SHARED SPACES

Creating an invitation to sit and stay a while is important in any home and for the boho chic home, with its holiday-resort vibe, that's even more so the case. Comfortable seating, outdoors and indoors, provides an opportunity to relax and reconnect.

With its strong focus on connection to nature, it's not surprising that the outdoor room is a central piece in this design style. Regardless of the amount of space you have, it's important to treat any outdoor space as an opportunity to create an addition to your boho sanctuary.

Outdoor spaces can include lounges, rugs, lamps and string lights, and plenty of soft furnishings. Plants (and more plants) and even artworks might feature in the outdoor room. These spaces are an extension of the home for relaxing with family and friends and enjoying life al fresco. Loved items picked up on global travels have a place throughout the boho home and are often featured in the outdoor room.

▸ Earthy touches complement the relaxing scene in this boho chic seating nook.

While there are guiding principles, boho chic is a style that's characterised by personal touches, and choice of decor is the perfect place for self-expression.

DECOR

▾ The mix of global textiles and plants in this scene speaks boho chic loud and clear.

Your choice of decorative items in the boho chic home is exactly that: your choice. This style is characterised by a highly individual approach to decor, often incorporating unique pieces from different cultures, vintage finds and handcrafted items that showcase a global aesthetic.

These items might be wall art – consider displaying a diverse collection in different formats, from paintings or photographs to macrame wall hangings or hanging plants, to nail the style. You can't really have enough plants, so complement hanging plants with larger varieties – lush green plants like ferns, Swiss cheese or rubber plants suit the vibe, as do cacti and succulents – to create an indoor-outdoor feel in the home.

For the finishing touches, consider statement candlesticks and candles, as well as incense holders.

Combine natural elements with a focus on comfort, and you'll be on track to create a beautiful boho chic space.

FURNISHINGS

When selecting furnishings for your boho chic home, it's important to focus first on natural elements – choose wood, wicker, bamboo and rattan for furniture and accessories to introduce that warm, organic feel to the home.

Comfort is also important in boho styling, and furniture that's characteristic of the style often has a low profile – think large, low-slung chairs or couches. Or a hanging rope chair if you have the space and inclination for it. Vintage and Asian-inspired furniture has a place too, with wooden stools or benches a common feature as well as functional items, such as butchers' blocks, printers' drawers or old tool boxes.

Try layering textures by choosing soft furnishings in wool, linen, cotton and velvet, and introducing patterns with geometric shapes on wall hangings, rugs, soft furnishings or decorative items.

▲ Oversized pendants in natural materials are iconic of boho chic styling.

Have fun styling your boho chic home through a combination of neutral backgrounds, comfortable furnishings and personal decorative touches.

MOOD BOARD

Creating a boho chic mood board is sure to be a fun and rewarding process. Once you've nailed your choice of (neutral) background, it's really all about comfort and personal taste – what a great combination to work with.

Build up your mood board by selecting your preferred furniture. These are usually the big-ticket items that will do much to set the tone of the home. Splurge if you can on a really comfy boho-style couch or hanging chair. Next, focus on the soft furnishings – rugs, curtains, throws and cushions. Layer with soft, natural textiles in geometric or ethnic patterns. These will do a lot to establish the boho chic vibe at your place.

Last but definitely not least, add some personal decorative touches that tell stories of your life and put them on display within the home.

◂ These plant pots feature geometric patterns with a global feel.

▴ This curved rattan bedhead is a perfect boho chic style piece.

▴ Global vibes are introduced by the decorative bowls and cushions on display here.

◂ Terracotta tiling is a cool and fresh touch to the boho chich home.

Earthy tones and natural materials and textiles abound in this lush boho chic bedroom.

Expansive and indulgent sums up this boho chic living space.

This home nails the 'wish you were here' aspect of the boho chic style.

It doesn't get more 'on trend' than Japandi, an easeful home style that unites the best elements of functional-and-cosy Scandi with earthy-and-minimal Japanese interior design.

JAPANDI

▸This bedroom perfectly encapsulates the serene mood of Japandi.

As the name suggests, it's a fusion: at the high level, a union of Japanese and Scandi design.

It's also a fusion of two concepts: *wabi-sabi* and *hygge*. Wabi-sabi, meaning finding the beauty in imperfection, in this context is about simplicity, connection to nature, and embracing minimalism by accepting the impermanence of 'things'. The message being: don't have too many of them! Hygge is by now well known, in interior design circles at least, as the Scandinavian term that connotes cosiness and intimacy in the home.

In terms of an aesthetic, Japandi bridges Scandinavian comfort and functionality with Japanese minimalism and style. Where Japanese interiors are sleek, Scandinavian ones are rustic. The rich, earthy colours of Japanese design help to keep the black and white palette of Scandinavian homes from feeling austere. Japandi is the perfect mix.

STYLE HIGHLIGHTS

TEXTURE

While the palette is earthy and neutral, and the overall aesthetic is minimal, texture is introduced through hard and soft furnishings in order to layer and create warmth and cosiness in the home.

CRAFTSMANSHIP

Traditionally, objects in the home would be hand-crafted for a specific job, and then used for that job. These objects should not be untouchable, but well enough made to stand the test of time. Quality: as far as budget and practicalities allow.

NATURAL MATERIALS

Warm woods and earthy materials sit at the heart of the home. The use of wood in particular is a major theme and it can appear in different contexts and shades. Natural materials such as linen, cotton and wool apply for furnishings.

SIMPLICITY

Uncluttered spaces and intentional choices of furniture, furnishings and decor that leans to the minimalist aesthetic underpin the idea of simplicity in Japandi design.

FUNCTIONALITY

A place for everything and everything in its place is a cliche that rings true in Japandi design. Here there is a strong sense of appropriateness, order and place, which combine to create ease and calm in the home.

INTENTION

There is a sense of balance and in the home, achieved through careful and intentional choice and positioning of elements. Nothing is left to chance. Choose all items, especially decorative pieces, with clarity of intention.

Let in as much light as possible to illuminate the beautiful, earthy, wooden features of your Japandi-styled home.

THE CANVAS

▾ Simplicity, elegance and natural materials are on display in every aspect of this dining scene.

Clean lines, serenity, an orderly yet approachable home. That's the goal of Japandi, so what's the right background canvas to help you achieve that look and feel in your home?

The first thing to consider is your choice of materials. Incorporating lots of wood and natural elements is a must for success with this style. Later you can layer on textiles and furnishings, but for the canvas, think earthy, natural and wooden elements as the backbone of the home.

Japandi-style homes are characterised by bright spaces with lots of natural light. Consider where the natural light source is in your home and plan how to work around it so it's unobstructed. Embrace natural light by removing heavy curtains and using sheers or light-coloured blinds. Install minimalistic pendant lights or floor lamps to create soft, warm lighting.

Keep it warm and earthy, while maintaining the Scandi approach of neutral background and pops of colour, inspired by nature.

COLOUR PALETTE

Next up, think about the colour scheme you would like to implement on the 'canvas' of the home, such as on the walls and ceilings through the use of paintwork and flooring. Whites, warmer shades of white, beiges and taupes help to establish a minimalist palette that allows other design details to stand out. These warmer neutrals will evoke the warmer, earthy feel of the Japandi style, as opposed to the cooler whites of Scandi.

You may also want to consider some special features, such as limewash wall finishes and rich, midtone wooden elements on door frames and feature panels, to deliver a sense of calm and ease and balance to a room.

Feature colours to add depth and warmth in the Japandi style are inspired by nature, so think rust, ochre, rainforest and sage greens, muddy blues and rich browns.

▲The colours in this Japandi-styled studio room perfectly echo those found in the natural world.

You know you've been successful when you feel at ease in the home. It's well organised and meticulously conceived – but still warm and inviting.

MOOD

▾ Simple, intentional styling choices create order, which creates calm.

Mood, in Japandi style, is where it's at. More than any individual detail or design choice, you'll know you've been successful in creating the essence of this style when you can feel the vibe at your place and it feels calm, easeful, harmonious, serene and tranquil. Sounds like a lot to expect from interior design perhaps, but it's eminently possible and you can achieve it by following the guidelines in this chapter.

The unique balance of minimalism and a focus on functionality, layered with the poetic and earthy touches of Japanese-influenced style, are the twin factors which deliver the mood of Japandi. It's muted and understated, but also somehow soft, warm and inviting. Furthermore it's clear, crisp and uncluttered. There's no better place to be, with yourself or with others, than in the well-executed Japandi-style home.

Choose items that will support your goal to live an easy, harmonious life. Beauty with purpose.

DECOR

In Japandi interior design you get to think a little differently in your choice of decor. Ask yourself, What styling decisions can I make to support a healthy and meaningful lifestyle? Choose those items, be they quality crockery, quality table linen or locally made vases. The idea is to prioritise objects you will use daily (not hide away in cupboards) so that you can enjoy your home to the fullest. Choose functional items like vases and mugs over decorative ones – think traditional Japanese ceramics, cosy Scandinavian throws or carefully chosen artwork.

In most Japandi-styled homes, you'll spot an earthy vase filled with greenery. That's the beginning of the story of uniting indoor and outdoor spaces that's so important to this style. Japanese aesthetics leans to bonsai plants or bamboo, while Scandinavian design emphasises plants like monstera or fiddle leaf fig. Take your pick.

▸ These pretty glass teacups are carefully placed, ready for quenching a thirst and sharing a chat.

Created from fusion, a coming together of philosophies, Japandi interior design is all about balance, the balance that's needed to live together in harmony.

SHARED SPACES

▸ This carefully curated nook presents an invitation to enjoy the serenity with a good book in hand.

Japandi is all about a 'bringing together' of elements. At its core it's a fusion of East and West, of wabi-sabi simplicity with hygge cosiness, of Japanese earthiness and Scandi functionality. The sum of these parts equals a home that is well organised, well balanced and well placed to live in harmoniously.

Japandi homes are inviting – whether you are a guest or a resident of the home, there is always a peaceful spot to sit, a pleasing cup to drink from and a cosy throw to nestle under.

To the resident of a Japandi-styled home come the benefits of minimalism and order. Everything is where it ought to be, making locating what's needed an easy, stress-free event. Clutter is kept to a minimum, ensuring that the mental load is lightened and the soul is primed for joy.

Embrace the beauty in having less and displaying less, and in the process of choosing only what you truly desire, that which will bring you joy.

FURNISHINGS

Intentionality and functionality are key in the approach to Japandi furnishings. Items are carefully chosen, with a focus on quality, form and function. Look for furniture that could serve a dual purpose – perhaps a stool can double as a side table or a bed can accommodate in-built storage, eliminating the need for another piece of furniture.

Focus on furniture with clean lines, and declutter objects in the home so that those lines can be emphasised.

To enhance the rustic, earthy look of the Japanese influence, be sure to choose organic textures like linen or cotton for bedding or throws. Consider Japanese-influenced artwork, combined with contemporary pieces for a fresh and chic perspective.

Most of all, minimise. Aim to find beauty in less, and enjoy the satisfaction that comes from knowing that all items have purpose.

▲ Note how the consistent colour palette in this arrangement creates a sense of order and calm.

Give expression to your mood through a carefully curated choice of furniture, furnishings and decorative elements.

MOOD BOARD

Since Japandi interior style is all about the mood, getting your mood board right is an important step in nailing the style.

Bear in mind the description in the mood section of this chapter: it's about harmony, balance and ease in the home. To that end, look out for furniture, furnishings and even decorative items that are functional as well as beautiful. Choose the things you really love, and let the rest go. A minimalist aesthetic is essential to creating the Japandi style.

Where budget allows, opt for artisan or handcrafted items that feel good as well as look good.

Warm woods and earthy tones, colours and objects inspired by nature should form the centrepiece of your Japandi mood board.

◂ Choose artwork with intention, taking inspiration from contemporary and Eastern influences.

▾ Cute decorative touches that make a nod to Japanese aesthetic work well in this style.

◂ The single stem in an oversized smoked glass vase is both minimal and impactful.

This large floral print is reminiscent of Japanese artists like Hokusai.

Earthy materials, textures and colours combine beautifully to create a stunningly simple bedroom.

Light, white and bright are hallmarks of Japandi home style.

HERRON

First Published in 2025 by Herron Book Distributors Pty Ltd
14 Manton St
Morningside
QLD 4170
www.herronbooks.com

Captain Honey

Custom book production by Captain Honey Pty Ltd
12 Station Street
Bangalow
NSW 2479
www.captainhoney.com.au

Cataloguing-in-Publication. A catalogue record for this book is available from the National Library of Australia

ISBN 978-1-923279-24-7

Image on front cover and page 37: Studio Noema.
Photography © Nat Spada.

Images on pages 76, 89 © Living4Media

Images on pages 43, 71, 137, 160, 201 © Stocksy

Images on pages 13, 24, 64 © Austock

All other images © Shutterstock

Printed and bound in China

5 4 3 2 1 25 26 27 28 29

COLLECT THE SERIES